You may think you know almost everything there is to know about the man you've chosen to be your groom. Trust us, this little book will show that really, you don't.

No matter how long you two have known each other, no matter how much you've talked—about matters both serious and foolish—there's plenty you haven't yet learned about him.

This hundred-question quiz will help you to educate yourself, so grab a pencil and see how you do. You won't find the answers in the book, of course. For those, you'll have to check with your man. When you do, you'll find yourselves talking *to* each other *about* each other: your likes and dislikes, your beliefs and opinions, and stories and facts about your pasts.

They're little things, sure, but they aren't insignificant. They're the bits and pieces that make up who we are. And knowing about them is much more than collecting mere personal trivia. Knowing is caring.

Score ten points for each correct answer (taking partial credit wherever you can) and rate yourself according to this scale:

Above 900: What a performance!
800-900: Very good for a couple just starting out.
600-790: Pretty good. You'll improve as time goes by.
Below 600: Ask your groom for a remedial course.

Good luck.

— D.C.

Do You KNOW Your GROOM?

by Dan Carlinsky

SOURCEBOOKS, INC.
NAPERVILLE, ILLINOIS

Published by Sourcebooks, Inc.
P.O. Box 4410, Naperville, Illinois 60567-4410
(630) 961-3900
Fax: (630) 961-2168
www.sourcebooks.com

Library of Congress Cataloging-in-Publication Data
Dan Carlinsky
Do you know your groom? / by Dan Carlinsky.
p. cm.
ISBN 13: 978-1-4022-0683-2
ISBN 10: 1-4022-0683-6

Printed and bound in the United States of America
SP 10 9 8 7 6

1. DOES YOUR GROOM KNOW HIS OWN CAR LICENSE PLATE NUMBER?

_____ Yes

_____ Almost

_____ Not even close

2. WHAT NICKNAMES HAS HE GONE BY, FROM CHILDHOOD ON?

_____

3. DOES HE THINK A GUY WHO GETS REGULAR MANICURES IS:

_____ Properly concerned about the health and appearance of his nails?

_____ Too vain?

_____ Not exactly Marines material?

4. HAS HE EVER TAKEN LESSONS ON A MUSICAL INSTRUMENT?

_____ Yes, he's studied the _____

_____ No

5. DOES YOUR GROOM THINK EATING DINNER IN BED IS:

_____ Great—he'd do it every day if he could?

_____ OK on rare occasions?

_____ Too messy even to contemplate?

6. WOULD HE RATHER:

_____ Play a board game?

_____ Go dancing?

_____ Explore a city he's never been to?

_____ Bike ride in the country?

7. IF HE WON A HUGE LOTTERY PRIZE, WHAT'S THE FIRST THING HE'D DO?

_____ Party

_____ Quit his job

_____ Start looking for a new house

_____ Find a financial advisor

8. IF HE FINDS HIMSELF AT A REALLY BAD MOVIE, WOULD HE RATHER:

_____ Leave?

_____ Sit it out and complain later?

9. IF SERVED RAW OYSTERS, WILL HE:

_____ Devour them?

_____ Pick at them?

_____ Turn them down?

_____ Hide them?

10. IS THERE A FAVORITE FAMILY RECIPE THAT YOUR GROOM
THINKS SHOULD BE PRESERVED FOR POSTERITY?

_____ Yes, his _____'s recipe for _____.

_____ No

11. HAS HE EVER KICKED A BAD HABIT?

_____ Yes, he stopped _____.

_____ No, he never has.

12. DOES YOUR GROOM CONSIDER A WALK ON THE
BEACH IN WINTER:

_____ Romantic?

_____ A waste of time?

14. CAN HE MANIPULATE A TV
REMOTE WITHOUT
LOOKING AT THE
BUTTONS?

_____ Easily

_____ If he feels around a
bit

_____ No

13. CAN HE TYPE WITHOUT
LOOKING AT THE KEYBOARD?

_____ Very well

_____ OK

_____ Not at all

15. DOES HE KNOW THE BIRTHDAYS OF AT LEAST SIX PEOPLE
OTHER THAN HIS IMMEDIATE FAMILY?

_____ Yes, at least that many

_____ No, but he does know a few

_____ He barely knows his own

16. DOES HE NOW KNOW, OR HAS HE EVER KNOWN:

_____ A circus performer?

_____ An orchestra conductor?

_____ A mobster?

_____ A TV weatherman?

17. WHEN WAS THE LAST TIME HE STAYED UP ALL NIGHT?

_____ Less than a week ago

_____ Less than a year ago

_____ It's been ages

_____ Probably never

18. DOES HE HAVE ANY HABITS NOW THAT HE'D LIKE TO BEAT?

_____ Yes, he wants to quit _____.

_____ No, he doesn't.

19. WHAT JUNK FOOD CAN'T HE STAY AWAY FROM?

_____

20. MOST DAYS, WOULD HE RATHER:

_____ Go to a party?

_____ Hang out with a couple of friends?

_____ Be by himself?

21. DOES HE THINK GIVING KIDS A FIRM BEDTIME IS:

_____ A must for a peaceful household?

_____ Impossible to enforce, so forget it?

_____ Unnecessary, since they'll go to sleep when they're tired?

22. IF YOU ASKED HIM, WOULD YOUR GROOM SPEND A SATURDAY MORNING GOING TO YARD SALES OR A CHURCH RUMMAGE SALE?

_____ Happily

_____ Only if dragged

_____ Only if drugged

23. WHICH CATEGORY OR CATEGORIES WOULD HE USE TO DESCRIBE HIMSELF IN HIGH SCHOOL?

_____ Prep

_____ Gang member

_____ Middle-of-the-roader

_____ Goth

_____ Freak

_____ Nerd

_____ Outsider

_____ Partygoer

_____ Jock

_____ Sports fan

24. SOMEONE CUTS IN FRONT OF THE TWO OF YOU IN A MOVIE LINE. WILL YOUR GROOM:

_____ Tell the intruder to get back where he belongs?

_____ Mutter quietly to you but say nothing?

_____ Pretend not to notice?

25. A FRIEND BORROWS $20 AND FORGETS TO PAY IT BACK. WILL HE:

_____ Remind the friend?

_____ Drop a hint?

_____ Keep silent to avoid embarrassing the friend?

_____ Forget about it himself?

26. IF ASKED TO NAME HIS ALL-TIME FAVORITE MOVIE, HE'LL SAY:

_____ "It's _____."

_____ "I can't choose just one."

_____ "I'm not a big moviegoer."

27. HE BELIEVES THAT DREAMS PREDICT THE FUTURE.

_____ Often

_____ Sometimes

_____ Never

28. WOULD HE BE A CONTESTANT ON A BIG-MONEY TV GAME SHOW?

_____ He'd do it in a flash.

_____ If you urged him to.

_____ You've got to be kidding!

29. OF THE PEOPLE FROM HIS PAST HE'S IN TOUCH WITH, OTHER THAN FAMILY, WHICH ONE HAS HE KNOWN THE LONGEST?

_____

30. DOES YOUR GROOM KNOW WHAT COLOR YOUR EYES ARE?

_____ Yes

_____ No, but he'll try to guess

_____ No way

31. WHAT'S HIS MOTHER'S MAIDEN NAME?

_____

32. DOES HE KNOW *YOUR* MOTHER'S MAIDEN NAME?

_____ Yes

_____ No

33. IF YOU ASK HIM TO RECITE "MARY HAD A LITTLE LAMB," HOW WILL HE DO?

_____ He'll recite it easily.

_____ He'll stumble but more or less get it right.

_____ He'll mess up.

34. OF ALL THE FEMALE TEACHERS HE EVER HAD, WHICH ONE DOES HE CONSIDER THE HOTTEST?

_____

35. WHAT DOES HE THINK OF WATCHING TELEVISION DURING MEALTIME?

_____ It's OK if others want to watch, too.

_____ It's OK anytime—let others talk among themselves if they don't want to watch.

_____ It's rude, distracting, and unacceptable.

36. TO START THE MORNING, DOES YOUR GROOM:

_____ Always want a big breakfast?

_____ Want at least a little something to eat?

_____ Happily start the day on an empty stomach?

37. IS HE COMFORTABLE EATING A FULL MEAL IN A RESTAURANT ALONE?

_____ He'll dine alone any time.

_____ He'll eat solo if necessary, but he'd prefer not to.

_____ He'd rather grab a candy bar from a vending machine.

38. IN THE BANK, AFTER THE TELLER COUNTS OUT HIS MONEY, DOES HE RE-COUNT IT? DOES HE DOUBLE-CHECK MONEY FROM AN ATM OR ACCEPT THE MACHINE'S COUNT? HOW ABOUT CHANGE FROM A STORE CLERK?

	COUNT	NO COUNT
TELLER		
ATM		
CLERK		

39. DOES HE GENERALLY AIM TO ARRIVE AT APPOINTMENTS:
_____ Ahead of time?
_____ Just on time?
_____ No more than a few minutes late?
_____ Whenever he gets there?

40. DOES YOUR GROOM:
_____ Slide his chair back under the table when he gets up?
_____ Close drawers, cupboard doors, and closet doors when he's done with them?
_____ Choose the piece of fruit that's getting dangerously close to overripe?

41. "WHAT HAPPENED TO THE GUY WHO RAN RIGHT THROUGH THE SCREEN DOOR?" "HE STRAINED HIMSELF." YOUR GROOM WILL JUDGE THIS JOKE:
_____ Worth a big laugh
_____ OK
_____ Much too, er, strained

42. APPLIANCE MANUALS AND WARRANTY CARDS—DOES HE:
_____ Keep them?
_____ Pitch them?

43. "NEVER DO BUSINESS WITH A FRIEND."
_____ He agrees.
_____ He disagrees.

44. WHICH OF THESE MAKE HIM VERY UNCOMFORTABLE?

_____ Small, enclosed spaces

_____ Being completely alone

_____ Large, out-of-control dogs

_____ Deep water

_____ The thought of growing old

45. HE HAS NIGHTMARES:

_____ Often

_____ Occasionally

_____ Rarely

_____ Never

46. ARE HIS EYES EQUAL IN STRENGTH OR IS ONE STRONGER?

_____ Equal

_____ The _____ eye is stronger.

47. WHEN TOLD ABOUT A MARRIED COUPLE WITH SEPARATE BEDROOMS, YOUR GROOM THINKS:

_____ If it works for them, fine.

_____ There's probably something wrong there.

_____ Who knows what goes on in other people's lives?

48. HE'S INVITED TO A DINNER PARTY AND OFFERED A CHANCE TO CHOOSE HIS TABLE PARTNER, KNOWING NOTHING BUT THE OCCUPATION OF EACH GUEST. WHICH OF THESE WOULD YOUR GROOM PICK TO SIT NEXT TO?

_____ Newspaper reporter
_____ Minister
_____ Firefighter
_____ Librarian
_____ Fish distributor

49. CAN HE:

_____ Jump rope?
_____ Spin a hula-hoop?
_____ Play jacks?

50. WHICH TYPE OF VEHICLE HAS HE EVER DRIVEN—EVEN ONCE?

_____ Convertible
_____ Bus
_____ Motorcycle
_____ Pickup
_____ Large truck

51. HOW DID HIS PARENTS MEET?

_____

52. WOULD HE RATHER TAKE VACATIONS TO:

_____ The same place over and over, for familiarity and comfort?

_____ Different places each time, for variety and adventure?

_____ Some of both?

53. HOW MANY OF *SNOW WHITE*'S SEVEN DWARFS CAN HE NAME?

_____ None

_____ One to three

_____ Four to six

_____ All seven (Happy, Grumpy, Dopey, Sleepy, Sneezy, Bashful, and Doc)

54. WHEN WAS HE LAST INSIDE A HOSPITAL, EITHER AS A PATIENT OR AS A VISITOR? EXPLAIN.

_____

55. DOES YOUR GROOM THINK HUSBANDS AND WIVES SHOULD HAVE A NIGHT OUT WITHOUT THEIR MATES:

_____ Often?

_____ Occasionally?

_____ Never?

56. AT THE BEACH, DOES HE PREFER:

_____ Lying in the sun?   _____ Walking on the rocks?

_____ Lying under an umbrella?   _____ None of them?

_____ Playing or walking on the sand?

57. AS A CHILD, DID HE EVER GO TO SUMMER CAMP? (TEN BONUS POINTS IF YOU CAN NAME THE CAMP—UNLESS YOU WENT THERE TOO.)

_____ Yes, he went to _____.

_____ No, he wasn't a camp-goer.

58. IF HE THOUGHT A REPAIRMAN HAD CHEATED HIM, WOULD HE:

_____ Keep quiet and pay?

_____ Point out the problem and ask that it be fixed?

_____ Loudly refuse to pay and make a fuss?

59. WHERE WERE HIS PARENTS BORN?

Mother: _____

Father: _____

60. THE LAST TIME HE WAS IN A FISTFIGHT WAS:

_____ This month

_____ This year

_____ Sometime during the past five years

_____ A long, long time ago, if ever

61. WHAT DOES HE THINK IS THE FUNNIEST SHOW CURRENTLY ON TV?

_____

62. DOES HE TRY TO ANSWER THE PHONE ON THE FIRST, SECOND, OR THIRD RING, OR DOES HE NOT COUNT?

_____ First
_____ Second
_____ Third
_____ Whichever

63. HAS HE EVER BEEN UNCONSCIOUS? WHY?

_____ Yes, because _____
_____ No

64. HAS HE EVER:

_____ Bungee jumped?
_____ Ridden an animal other than a horse?
_____ Been a pallbearer?
_____ Twirled pizza dough in the air?

65. WHICH SPORT HAS HE *NEVER* PLAYED, EVEN ONCE?

_____ Soccer
_____ Lacrosse
_____ Golf
_____ Softball
_____ He's played all of these

66. WHAT'S HIS MOST MEMORABLE CHILDHOOD VACATION?

_____

67. "A MEAL WITHOUT DESSERT ISN'T REALLY A MEAL." YOUR GROOM WOULD:

_____ Agree

_____ Disagree

68. WITHIN TWO, HOW MANY KEYS DOES HE USUALLY CARRY?

_____

69. DOES HE KNOW HOW MANY RINGS HIS MOTHER WEARS?

_____ Yes

_____ No

70. DOES HE ENJOY:

_____ Walking barefoot?

_____ Watching a rodeo?

_____ Listening to gospel music?

_____ Climbing trees?

71. HAS HE EVER KNOWN ANYONE WITH ONE OF THESE NICKNAMES?

_____ Fats   _____ Baldy   _____ Red

_____ Peanut   _____ Pinky   _____ Moose

72. HAS HIS NAME EVER APPEARED IN A NEWSPAPER HEADLINE?

_____ Yes, because _____.

_____ No, but it's been in an article.

_____ No, but he's written a letter to the editor that's been published.

_____ No, never.

73. HAS HE EVER HAD A BOSS HE TRULY LIKED AND
RESPECTED? WHO?
_____ Yes: _____
_____ Never

74. DOES HE CONSIDER HIMSELF:
_____ A good joke teller?
_____ Not much of a teller but a good critic?
_____ Not really a joke person?

75. WHICH OF THESE CAN HE LOCATE?
_____ The Parthenon
_____ Mont Saint Michel
_____ Monticello
_____ Pamplona
_____ None of 'em

76. DOES YOUR GROOM THINK DOGS AND CATS:
_____ Should never be fed table scraps?
_____ Can be fed from the table, at least occasionally?

77. IN HOT WEATHER, WHICH DOES HE PREFER?
_____ Air conditioning
_____ Fans
_____ Toughing it out

78. DURING THE PAST YEAR, HAS HE CONSIDERED GROWING A BEARD OR MUSTACHE? IF HE HAS ONE, HAS HE CONSIDERED SHAVING IT?

_____ He's toyed with the idea.

_____ The thought hasn't crossed his mind.

79. DURING THE PAST YEAR, HAS HE CONSIDERED GETTING A TATTOO? IF HE HAS ONE, HAS HE CONSIDERED HAVING IT REMOVED?

_____ He's toyed with the idea.

_____ The thought hasn't crossed his mind.

80. TWO YEARS BEFORE YOU DECIDED TO MARRY, WOULD HE HAVE GUESSED THAT HE'D BE GETTING ENGAGED WITHIN THAT TIME PERIOD? HOW ABOUT ONE YEAR BEFORE?

	2 YEARS	1 YEAR
ABSOLUTELY		
MAYBE		
NO WAY		

81. DOES HE REMEMBER MUCH ABOUT YOUR FIRST DATE TOGETHER?

_____ Yes, in great detail.

_____ He remembers a little about it.

_____ The event is gone from his memory.

82. IS THERE ANY HOUSEHOLD CHORE THAT YOUR GROOM ACTUALLY ENJOYS?

_____ Yes: _____

_____ None whatsoever

83. WHEN ASKED AS A CHILD WHAT HE WANTED TO BE WHEN HE GREW UP, HE ANSWERED:

_____

84. WHERE DOES HE USUALLY CARRY HIS WALLET? (TEN BONUS POINTS IF YOU KNOW WHAT COLOR IT IS.)

_____

85. FOOLING AROUND IN AN OFFICE, HAS HE EVER PHOTOCOPIED A PART OF HIS BODY?

_____ Glad to say, he hasn't.

_____ Sorry, he has.

86. DOES HE HAVE A BOYHOOD FRIEND WHO HAS BECOME:

_____ A clergyman?

_____ A rock musician?

_____ A railroad conductor?

_____ A grade school teacher?

_____ A policeman or security guard?

87. WHAT'S HE BETTER AT?

_____ Darts   or   _____ Ping Pong
_____ Omelets   or   _____ Scrambled Eggs
_____ Hearing   or   _____ Smelling

88. DOES YOUR GROOM HAVE A SCAR ANYWHERE OTHER THAN ON HIS FACE OR ARMS?

_____ Yes, on his _____
_____ Not a one

89. IF HE HAD A TWELVE-YEAR-OLD DAUGHTER WHO NEEDED HER VISION CORRECTED AND COULD HAVE EITHER EYEGLASSES OR CONTACTS, WHICH WOULD HE URGE HER TO WEAR? WHAT ABOUT A SON?

	DAUGHTER	SON
EYEGLASSES		
CONTACTS		

90. DOES HE KNOW PIG LATIN?

_____ Esyay
_____ Onay

91. HAS HE EVER WATCHED TELEVISION OR BEEN ONLINE:

_____ For more than four hours straight?
_____ For more than eight hours straight?
_____ For more than twelve hours straight?

92. DOES HE THINK HE LOOKS HIS BEST:
_____ In casual clothes?
_____ Dressed up?
_____ In nothing at all?

93. HOW MANY VEGETARIANS DOES HE KNOW?
_____ None or one
_____ Two to five
_____ More than five

94. DOES HE HAVE ANY FORMER FRIENDS THAT HE NOW INTENTIONALLY AVOIDS? WHO?
_____ Yes: _____
_____ No

95. DOES YOUR GROOM HAVE ANYTHING THAT WAS ONCE OWNED BY ONE OF HIS GRANDPARENTS? BY ONE OF HIS GREAT-GRANDPARENTS?
_____ Yes, a grandparent's _____
_____ Yes, a great-grandparent's _____
_____ Nothing

96. HOW WELL DOES HE REMEMBER PHONE NUMBERS? DOES HE KNOW:
_____ His family's number from his childhood?
_____ Any number he had in a school dormitory?
_____ The first number he had of his own?
_____ The number at his first full-time job?

97. DOES HE KNOW WHO CHARLIE PARKER WAS?

_____ Sure: the bebop-era alto sax player.

_____ No, he knows very little about jazz.

98. WHICH RELATIVE OR GOOD FRIEND DRIVES HIM THE CRAZIEST?

_____

99. HOW MANY ARTICLES OF CLOTHING DOES HE HAVE THAT ARE MORE THAN SIX YEARS OLD?

_____ None

_____ At least one

_____ Several

_____ Pretty much his whole wardrobe

100. "THE BEST RESTAURANT MEAL IN THE WORLD ISN'T AS ENJOYABLE AS A GOOD MEAL AT HOME." WOULD HE:

_____ Agree?

_____ Disagree?

_____ Say "Well, that depends…"?